Composting—\

Susan Hughes

Do you ever wonder what goes on in a compost pile? Let's listen in on a conversation among some creatures who live in a compost pile.

Worm 1: Well, it's another beautiful day in the compost pile. Time to get to work to make the world a better place!

Worm 2 (*yawning*): I'm too hungry to make the world a better place. Let's eat first.

Worm 1: Exactly! Eating and digesting is just how we *do* make the world a better place.

Worm 2: Are you joking?

Worm 1: Nope. Let me explain.

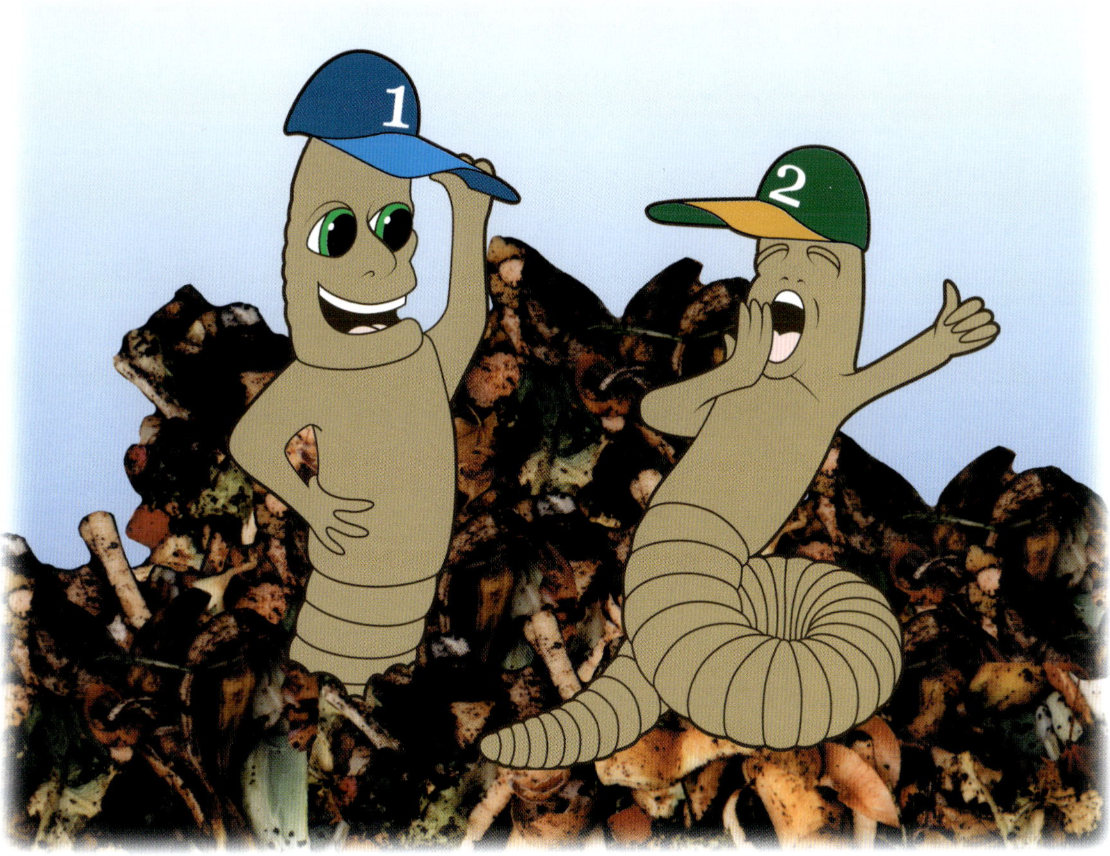
1
2

Worm 1: This is a compost pile. People toss in dead leaves, grass clippings, and food scraps such as banana peels, potato skins, and orange rinds. Sometimes they even add pet hair!

Worm 2: Why?

Worm 1: All these things used to be alive and growing. But all living things die. That's where we come in. We are decomposers, and along with some pals, we help these things break down—in other words, rot, or "decompose."

Worm 2: How?

Worm 1: We eat and digest them. The waste our worm bodies make is called "castings." These castings are full of great material for helping plants grow.

1

Worm 2: Good for us! But you said that our pals help, too. So, this compost pile is like a big restaurant!

Worm 1: Exactly. There are lots of diners here who, like us, are decomposers.

Worm 2: Yes, it is a little crowded in here, isn't it?

Worm 1: But that's okay. We don't all eat the same things! Here are some other decomposers: red worms, nematodes, and other earthworms—like us. Many kinds of worms eat decaying plants and vegetables and microbes. All our castings help the soil stay rich.

Red worms, nematodes, and other earthworms: Hello! Hello!

Nematode: I'm tiny. There can be 90,000 nematodes in one rotting apple!

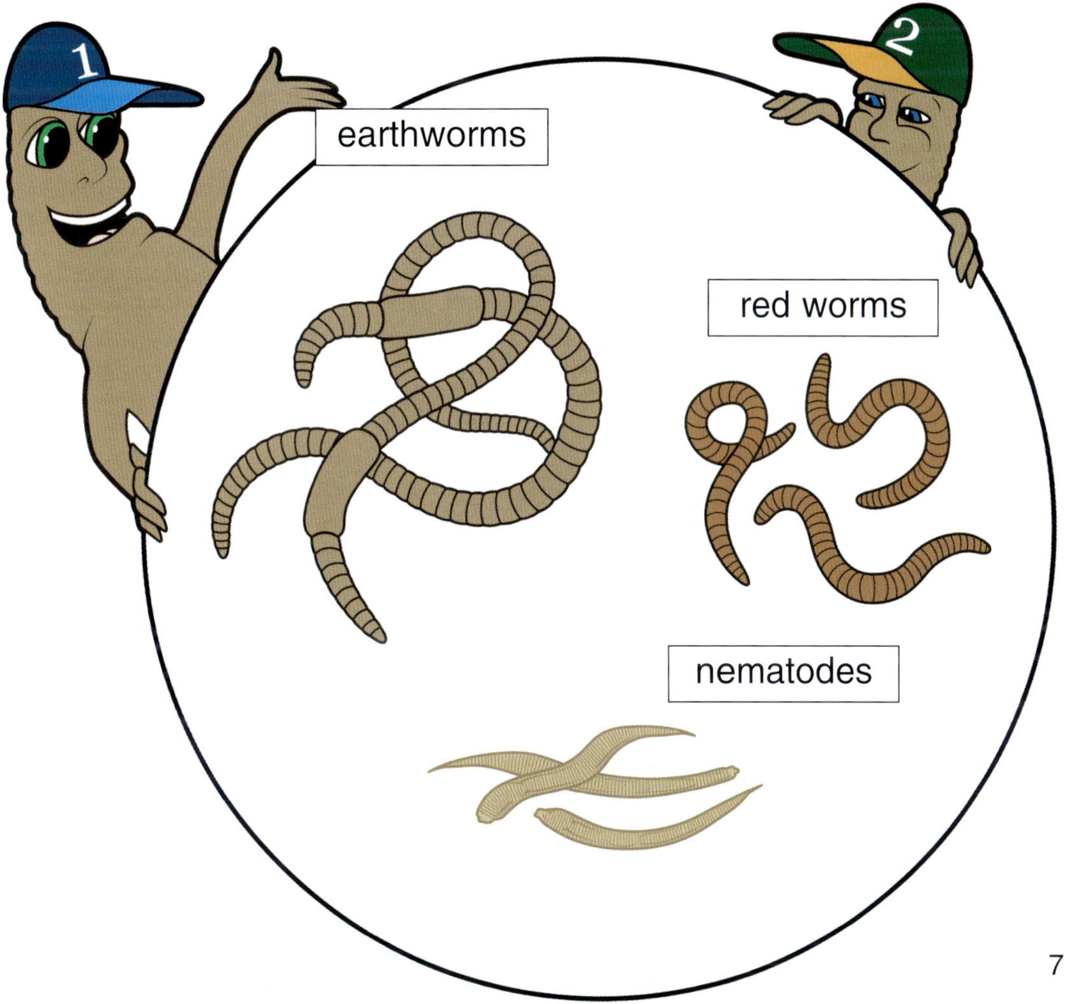
1
2
earthworms
red worms
nematodes

Worm 1: Here are more of our pals—some millipedes, sow bugs, snails, and slugs.

Millipedes, sow bugs, snails, and slugs: Hello!

Worm 1: These guys eat the same things we do. And, like us, they also shred plant material. That makes it easier for the bacteria and fungi to dig in.

Bacteria: We are the smallest living organisms.

Fungi: Some of us are molds. We are gray and white—and fuzzy!

Worm 2: Hi!

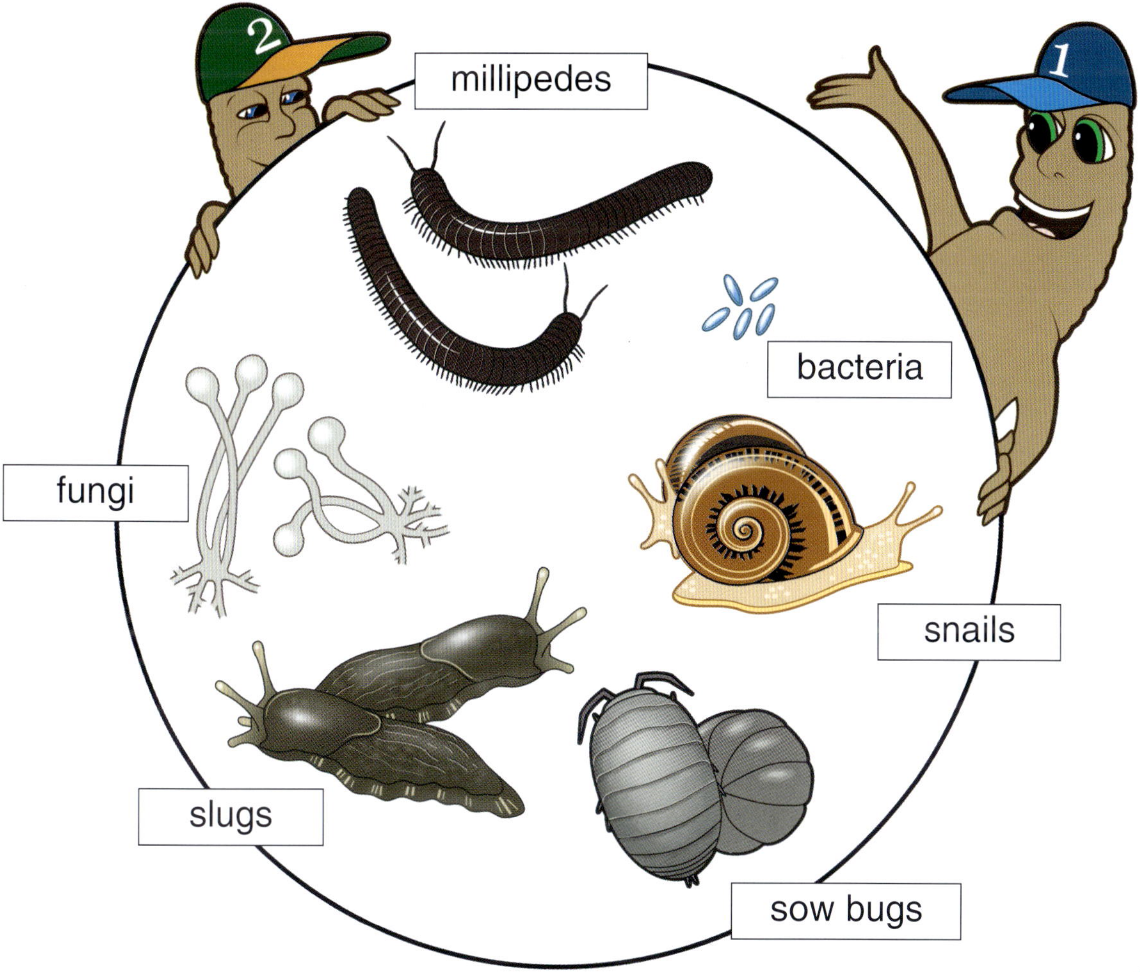
2
1
millipedes
bacteria
fungi
snails
slugs
sow bugs

Worm 1: And then we have the springtails and mites. Some eat fungi and decomposing plants. Some eat nematodes, eggs, and insect larvae.

Mites: Sometimes we hitch a ride on a fast beetle!

Springtail: I don't have wings. I jump when something bothers me.

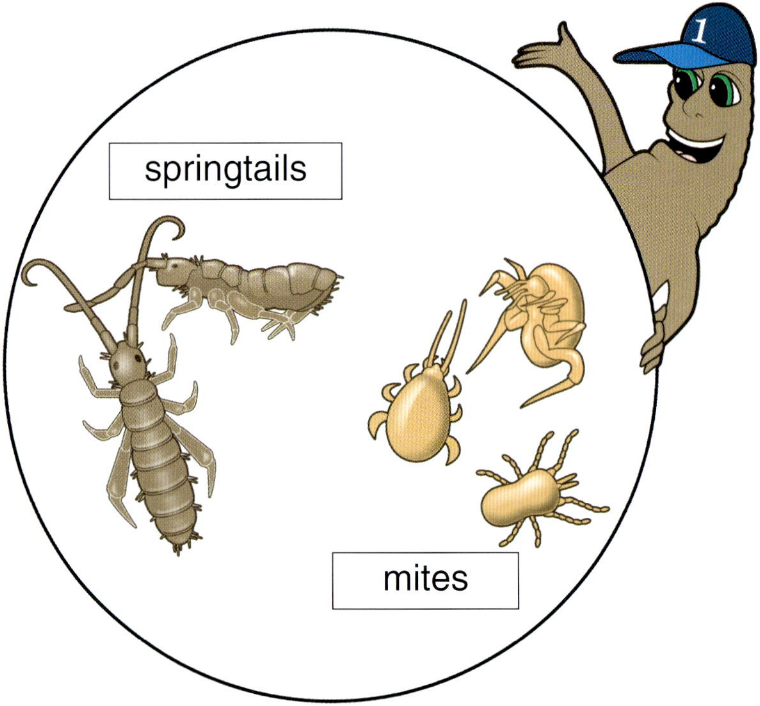

Worm 1: And then there are the organisms that eat springtails and mites. Here are some centipedes, carpenter ants, and beetles.

Centipedes, carpenter ants, and beetles: Pleased to meet you.

Centipede: I have poison glands in my claws. I poison and feed on newly hatched earthworms, small red worms, insects, and spiders.

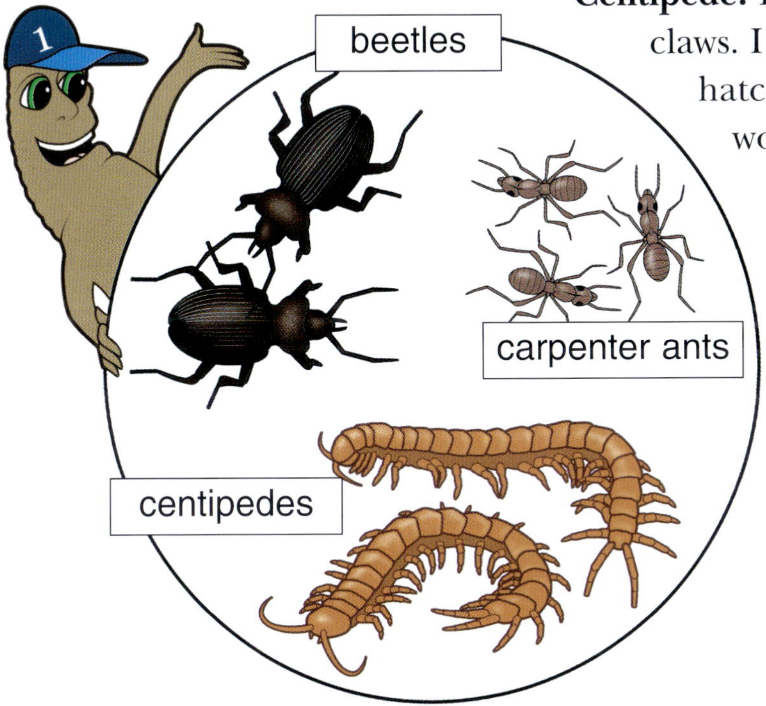

Worm 2: So, the compost heap is a big food web.

Worm 1: Everything is food for something else! And in the end, everything gets used up. Nothing is wasted. Everything and everybody returns to the soil, so even the plants are happy. They use the nutrients in the soil as food!

Worm 2: That means that we decomposers are great recyclers!

Nutrients are absorbed by plant roots and are taken up through the stem to the leaves.

Worm 1: We decomposers are good at our jobs—making compost—but we can sure use help from humans.

Child (*overhearing*): Great! What can we do?

Worm 1: You can make a small compost container in your kitchen. You will need …

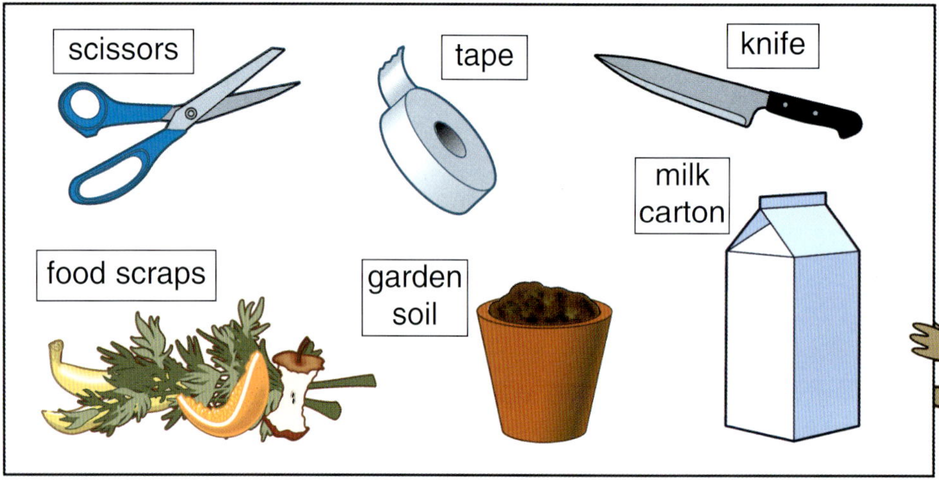

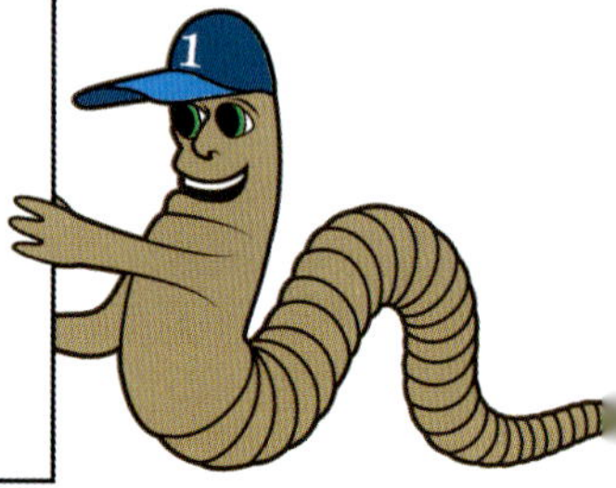

Child: What do I do?

Worm 1: Tape shut the open end of the milk carton. Then ...

Worm 2: ... with an adult's help ...

Worm 1: ... cut a flap on the top side of the carton.

Worm 1: Cut vegetable and fruit leftovers into small pieces ...

Child: ... with an adult's help.

Worm 2: Scatter them inside the carton.

Worm 1: Spread a little soil on top. There are bacteria and other decomposers in the soil that will begin to feed on the scraps. Every day, stir it up. Add some more scraps and soil.

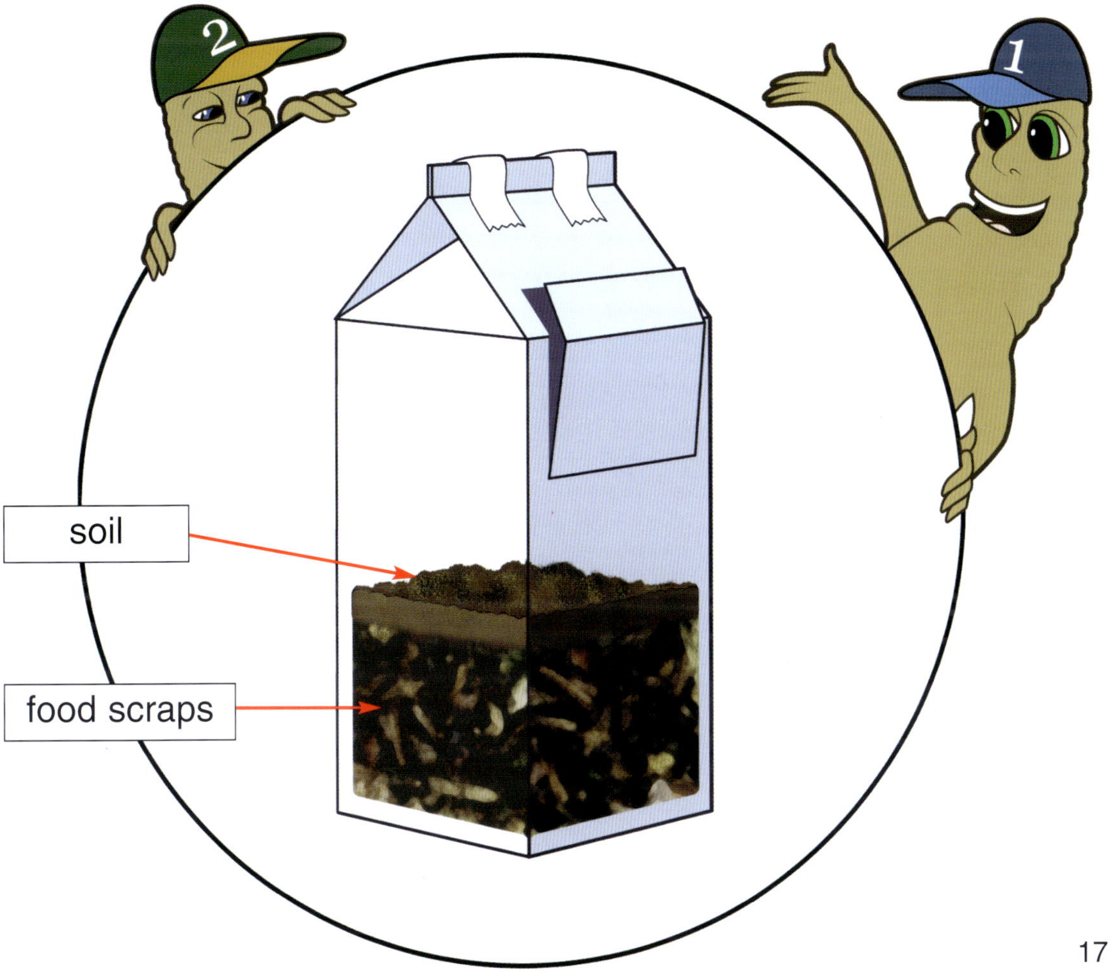
soil
food scraps

Worm 1: Stop adding scraps and soil when the carton is almost full.

Child: Will it explode?

Worm 1: No, but if you leave some space at the top, it's easier to stir. Stir each day for three more weeks.

Worm 2: Add a little water if it gets really dry.

Worm 1: When the soil is dark brown, you know the decomposers have done their job. They have turned the soil into compost, or "humus."

Worm 2: Spread the compost around your plants. They'll love the nutritious treat.

1
2

Worm 1: You can make compost outdoors, too. Buy a large compost bin or make some holes in a garbage can ...

Worm 2: ... with an adult's help.

Worm 1: Save vegetable and fruit scraps to load it up. Add some leaves and soil once in a while.

Child: And a little water.

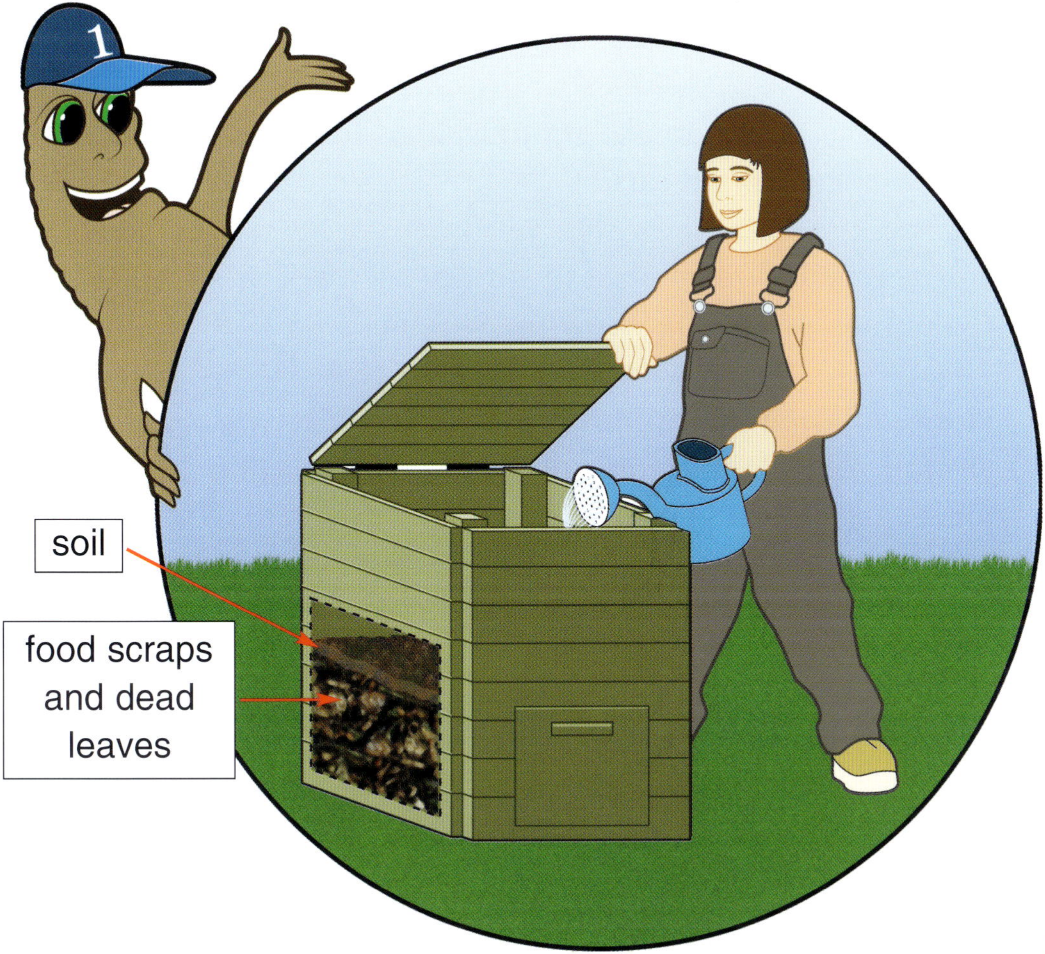
1
soil
food scraps and dead leaves

Worm 1: Don't put in any meat or fat ...

Worm 2: ... or you might get unwanted four-legged visitors, such as racoons and rats!

Worm 1: And don't forget to stir once a week or so. Decomposers like the extra air.

Worm 2: When the humus is dry and dark brown, spread it around your plants. Nutrients in the humus will help the plants grow!

2
1

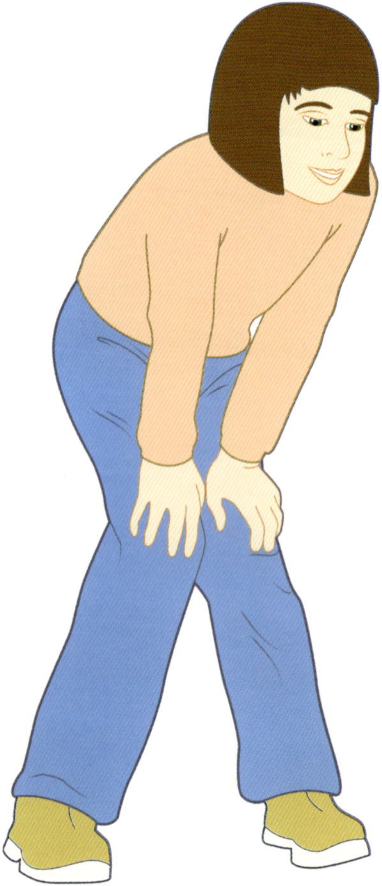

Worm 1: When you help us decomposers to make compost, you can feel proud ...

Worm 2: ... that you are helping the soil and the plants.

Worm 1: We are pleased to announce that you are now an official Super-Composter!

Child: Cool!

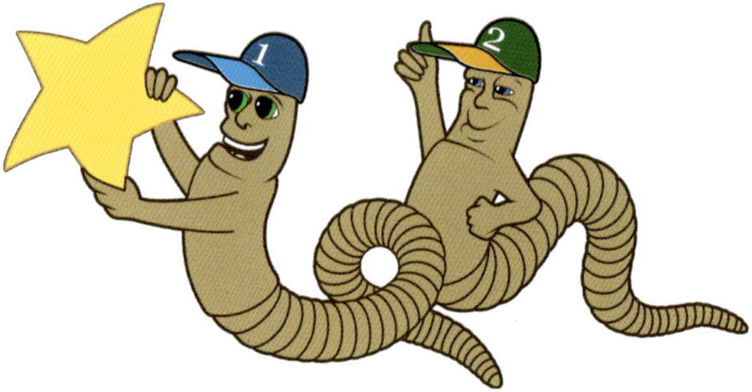